Christian lessons from dogs

Inspirational Tales of Friendship, Laughter, and Loyalty

Authors Name: Jennifer Chalaine

TABLE OF CONTENT

INTRODUCTION

This Bible study was provided purely as a subject for thought and prayer. Even if dogs may seem like a trivial subject, keep in mind that God gave His inspiration for every word in the Bible. Every verse in the Bible is inspired by God and is useful for teaching, rebuking, correcting, and training in righteousness (2 Timothy 3:16). Both Jesus and none of the disciples ever had a pet. Since Jesus was their perfect example and they all valued people above animals, we ought to view the world similarly. Animals should never take precedence over people.

Most people have never given much thought to what the Bible says about dogs, but as the aforementioned verses demonstrate, dogs are not among the Lord's top picks of living things. The Lord equates dogs with pigs, murderers, idolaters, witches, prostitutes, homosexuals, gore, violence, wickedness, worthlessness, folly, greed, deceit, and corrupt religious figures that relish destroying the souls of the defenseless. There are approximately fifty verses in the Bible that portray dogs, jackals, wild dogs, wolves, hyenas, and other canines negatively. There is not a single word that speaks positively about dogs. Not a single scripture describes dogs as domestic pets, with the exception of those kept by sinful people. Dogs were made to be scavengers, just like vultures, to clean up rotting corpses, according to the scriptures. Even when walking on a leash, a dog will naturally pick up any food that is dropped on the ground. Dogs will consume rotting food, which other carnivores will not touch.

Although the Lord does not expressly forbid dog ownership, it is heavily implied. Dog ownership may not be wrong, but idolizing your pet, whether it be a dog or another animal, is sin. Many Christians, who would shudder at the concept of idolatry, unknowingly worship their dogs. Some people who are called to serve in the mission field refuse to go since it would entail leaving their dog behind. Some people substitute the artificial urge to obtain affection from their pets for the natural human need to be loved. Some dog owners consent to the disruption of home gatherings by their pets. Some folks view their dogs as replacement "children."

Some dogs moan and yell until they get attention, just like spoiled children. More time is frequently spent playing with dogs than reading the Bible or praying. People who profess to adore Jesus wouldn't sacrifice their dog for Him, though. All of that is idolatry, and hundreds of Christians would have to turn from idolizing their dogs or other animals. Never should we place anyone or anything ahead of the Lord since doing so disqualifies us from being the Lord's disciple (Luke 14:26).

Put away all things of the world and follow the Lord's narrow path if you and I are sincere about seeking to please Him (Matthew 7:13 & 14). Souls are not saved by dogs. It is impossible for dogs to share the good news of salvation. Dogs have no spiritual significance. We must turn to the Lord and accept His love if we wish to feel love. As Christians, it is our duty to proclaim the gospel, serve and glorify God, and to love people—especially other Christians. The Kingdom of God does not benefit from dog ownership. The Bible declares that while everything is permissible for me, not everything is good for me and does not edify (1 Corinthians 10:23).

Chapter one

Lessons for Christian life from a dog!

Caleb, according to God, was a guy who completely obeyed him. The word "Caleb" is really canine. Caleb was chasing after his owner like a dog. Being close to his owner makes a dog ecstatic.

1. Dog never leaves his master's side.

Caleb, according to God, was a man who completely followed him, just as a dog completely follows its master. Being close to his owner makes a dog ecstatic. His constant preoccupation is his master, never toys, tricks, or playing. God thought of you before He created you. God invests His time and resources in us in the same way that we are enamored with our pets and give them our time and money. Unlike a puppy, we are frequently lured with shiny and alluring goods, but these rewards pale in comparison to our father's love and affection. He is to be our greatest love. He LOVES having you here. You are commanded to delight in Him, adore Him, and be enthralled by Him.

2. Dogs follow their masters wherever they go.

Caleb chose to follow the Lord rather than the Promised Land. More than any geographical location, he desired God. Your passions take control no matter how difficult life becomes, and if God is not your passion, you will drift away. God wants you to follow Him in all of your circumstances, whether they are good or bad. Never let your heart lead you astray; instead, follow God with your heart, and your heart will not depart from you. A dog will follow without asking any questions and with complete faith. In the same way, we must obey God and completely rely on His guidance.

3. Dogs don't see; they navigate by scent.

The sense of smell of dogs is far superior to that of humans. It is a thousand to a million times better than ours. Joshua could smell victory even though the other ten spies saw giants as they entered the Promised Land because he was guided by faith rather than sight. Following God makes us more like him, and he has supernatural vision into the future. You will develop your spiritual senses as you walk with God. We are instructed to walk by faith, not by sight, because of this.

4. Dogs are tolerant and forgetful.

No matter what you do to him, they cannot be angry for more than 30 seconds. Your circumstances do not determine your quality of life. Being unwilling to forgive others is a bitter root that eventually pushes you away from the master you should be serving. Regardless of the circumstances we are facing, we have the ability to choose to be happy.

5. You can train a dog.

Every dog has the potential to be a wonderful dog, but it takes training to unlock that potential. You don't automatically become loving and obedient, but you can. Learning involves forming those facts into who we are and educating ourselves to hold them. Everything in your life will be used for your training if you love God. You will become dissatisfied and doubt God if you do not love Him and obey His calling. We cannot accept our calling without preparation, just as the prodigal son and King Saul were not ready for it.

Chapter two

Seven Things Dogs Teach Us About God

My two dogs, Coco, a 4-year-old poodle mix who was rescued, and Brody, a 5-year-old golden retriever who we've had since he was a puppy, never cease to amaze me with their lessons from God. I'm learning the following things, to name a few:

unwavering love: Dogs accept and love us for who we are. They don't give a damn about our intelligence, what we're wearing, or whether we did poorly in school. They simply give us a kind gaze before curled up peacefully at our side. As God loves us, He commands us to love one another. A close second, in my opinion, would be to love one another as much as our pets do.

Total faith: My pets don't worry about where they will get their next meal or if I will be around to take care of them. I can certainly fail to live up to their expectations, but they don't appear to be aware of this. They put all of their love, faith, and trust in my husband and I, and they have complete faith in us. It's the kind of faith we ought to have in God, who genuinely never disappoints us.

Enjoy the little things: Brody, my golden retriever, enjoys nothing more than a game of fetch. His excitement knows no bounds when I pull out a ball and start throwing it for him. My dogs enjoy tiny moments like going on walks, chasing a bird in a field, and sniffing a variety of items along a route without giving any thought to life's anxieties or concerns. They accurately reflect Jesus' advice to not worry about tomorrow since it will take care of itself (Matt. 6:34, NIV).

We're never alone: If you own a dog, you'll never experience loneliness. I never have to come home to an empty house, not even when my husband needs to travel for work. There are always my dogs, who are happy to see me. Dogs are devoted friends during the years we are fortunate to have them, but God provides us with friendship that lasts forever.

Patience: My pets hang around for me all the time. We walk every day, although our routine is far from predictable. They will have to wait till I can schedule the time each day in between my obligations. They wait patiently for the appropriate moment to approach me rather than bugging or bothering me. We must wait for God's timing as well, but alas, I'm not always as patient as my pets.

Tolerance: Despite what my dogs think, I'm not a really good guy. Even when I occasionally "lose my temper," fail to pay attention to them, or ignore a need they have, it never appears to have an impact on their love and loyalty for me. They never hold it against me and are always forgiving of my flaws. If only we could be as understanding with one another!

Insecurity and dread were present when my dog Coco was brought to us after being rescued from a hoarding situation. I showed her a lot of love and care by treating her with kindness and gentleness. She eventually reacted to my efforts. She still gets anxious around others, but compared to many other dogs I've had, she has more faith in and loyalty to me. She serves as a reminder that God is love, and love triumphs.

Chapter three

Joshua 14:6-15, Lessons from a Dog

There are numerous lessons we can learn from dogs. The Bible mentions an extraordinary dog. Caleb is an acronym for "a dog," but it also stands for "a big heart." Isn't a big heart the same as a dog? Egypt was Caleb's birthplace. He was present when Moses assumed command of Israel and guided them across the Red Sea. One of the 12 spies sent to scout out the Promised Land to provide an early report on the challenges the Israelites would confront was Caleb. Ten of the spies came back with a negative report and terrified the populace by telling them about the giants and hurdles. 13:31.

Only Joshua and Caleb, who both supplied positive reports, spoke, with Joshua appearing to be silent: READ Num. 14:6-9. Let the dog be held accountable! Who answered the people? Caleb the stone... God's answer to Caleb's rejection of his knowledge was to let Israel wander another 40 years in the wilderness before entering the promised land, with Joshua and Caleb being the only exceptions. Num. Read the caption for Caleb's life at 14:24.

Josh, let's move on to the passages from today. 14:6-15. Joshua is 85 years old, and the God's promises from many years ago are now being fulfilled. Caleb is like a loyal dog waiting for the master; if my math is right, he was roughly 20 when he was a spy. Although Caleb was never in charge, he was always trustworthy and a kind person; the world needs a lot more people exactly like him. Caleb has three qualities that are important to take into account: 1) his loyalty; 2) his reliance on God for his needs; and 3) his innermost secret.

Caleb is devoted. We need individuals in our life who, like a devoted dog who never leaves, quietly walk with the Lord, are dependable, and are sincere. This is Caleb, sometimes known as "a dog." The Bible claims that he has a unique spirit and something unique about him. devoted service to God. He could always be reached.

As we undergo transformations, we require stable individuals in our life. Like a dog, devoted, trustworthy, and with a strong inner character. Caleb is a dog with a big heart. I am so appreciative of the people in my life that are devoted to God rather than to me. Dogs simply know how to love at all time and be nice to people. One of the first things that come to mind when you think of a dog would be loyalty. The world needs devoted individuals. For Josh. Caleb is alluding to the time when he was one of the 12 spies in 14:7-8. READ. This verse contains the word "convictions." Find devoted companions who share your convictions when your faith is faltering or you are terrified. I really value discussing issues with the elders and getting their encouragement to try our best to act morally. I value hearing their convictions about what we think to be God's priorities—not what will satisfy people.

I can only hope that my life can someday be described as wholehearted, but Caleb is a guy who lives his life with conviction, honesty, and wholeheartedness. Looking back on his life, Caleb is willing to accomplish everything the Lord asks of him, whether it be carrying grape clusters or taking on giants. Caleb is devoted to the Lord, and his life motto may easily be, "Lord, not my will, but yours." What we require is that. I don't need to be surrounded by those who are devoted to me, but rather to the Lord, the master.

Caleb was like a puppy waiting at the door for the master to return home—loyal, consistent, and real. You are fortunate when you come across a Caleb.

Caleb had no other source of support but the Lord. There are vicious dog owners in this world, but Caleb seemed unconcerned. God is his true master. He entirely surrendered his life to God. If you fully obey God, God will fully provide for you. When President Reagan was shot, I recall watching on television and being astounded by how quickly the secret service agents moved to put themselves in harm's way. Caleb would be in this. I was prepared to do anything the Lord asked of me. A specific merchant complained to Queen Elizabeth that doing her business would damage his own when she sent him to Holland.

Caleb received a long and active life. At the age of 85, he was still physically fit and capable of taking on giants (READ Josh. 14:10-11, 14). I am extremely grateful for believers who experience the joy and contentment of the Lord even in their final years. As Simeon, the dying man who carried the infant Jesus in the temple, said, "Sovereign Lord, as you have promised, you now dismiss your servant in peace, for my eyes have seen your salvation," I can hear Caleb echoing those words (Luke 2:29). Caleb is totally dependent on the Lord, who will mold his life in whichever way He sees fit.

God provided for Caleb. He was given land as payment and a seat of honor. If you do the arithmetic, Caleb was 20 years older than the next-oldest person, Joshua included, at the age of 85. He was undoubtedly a respected elder in the neighborhood. The principle that counts is: Follow God fully, and God will fully provide for you. Caleb's life is not a prescription for how the Lord will provide for us.

Whatever is in your heart will come out in your life, according to someone who once said, "Everything acts according to the spirit that is in it." Many people tell me what they think I want to hear, but with time, I learn who they really are and what spirit they possess. This is why the test of time is so crucial. No light comes from a lamp. Why? It isn't oiled. A second lamp illuminates a dim cubicle. Why? It is drenched in oil. You will release whatever is inside of you. Getting a new Spirit is the only true method to start a new life. And only God can be the source of the Holy Spirit! God is giving you a new Spirit, a whole transformation.

On Easter, I asked all who were receptive to hearing to stand: "If there are any here who need a new heart, Lord, show them the path, use Christian friends...seek forgiveness."

Caleb is a canine. Let's take a cue from dogs. A dog is devoted. The best Master of all is our Master, Jesus Christ. If you fully obey God, God will fully provide for you. He will reward you, even if it means making you perform challenging duties for him. A fresh Spirit is the key. In order for people in your world to describe you as different, may you accept and receive the Spirit of God. Amen.

Chapter four

Is dog also a creation of God yes or no?

Everything is known to God. The creatures and plants He placed on Earth were those that would serve His purposes the best when He created the planet. The Bible says that all land-dwelling animals were created by God on day six of Creation (Genesis 1:24). That indicates one on day six, God created dogs, or what we would refer to as the "dog kind." We use the term "kind" because God did not create all of the many canine breeds on that day. He did not develop the breeds of dogs we see today, including Chihuahuas, German Shepherds, pugs,

Dalmatians, and others. Instead, God made a single type of dog or a small number of various types of dogs, each of which has the genetic material (or DNA) necessary to develop into a specific breed.

DNA is a type of unique code that is present in every animal. The color, height, number of limbs and legs, and other physical traits of the animal are all determined by its DNA. A black dog may contain information in its DNA to be the color red, white, brown, or black, but only the black code is activated. This means that in every animal, "more" information than is "expressed" in the animal. For this reason, a black mother dog can give birth to pups that are brown, white, red, or spotted. Each color's code may be present in her DNA.

Say you wanted a dog that was always brown. How did we end up with only brown dogs? The solution is rather straightforward. We simply cross a brown dog with a brown dog. In the event that those two-produce black, brown, or red puppies, we simply select the brown ones and breed them to brown dogs. We can eliminate the DNA coding for black, red, or white by repeating this procedure frequently enough to produce only brown dogs.

But take note of what took place. We began with a dog that carried the genetic material necessary to produce any color, including black, brown, red, and white. We ultimately had dogs with lost the ability to distinguish between black, white, red, and any other color after we kept choosing the brown ones. No more DNA code or data was sent to us. In truth, we misplaced the data. Dogs are said to have evolved over millions of years from lower living forms by those who believe in evolution, thus it's crucial to understand this. Dogs can evolve and acquire new DNA codes, according to evolutionists, who assert that all the diverse kinds of dogs are proof of this. However, that isn't the situation at all.

Actually, the various dog breeds serve as evidence that evolution was not possible. Here's why: According to the Law of Biogenesis, all animals are descended from other members of their own species. Therefore, puppies, kittens, and snakes are all descended from their respective mothers, which are dogs, cats, and snakes, respectively. But according to evolutionists, a "non-dog" gave birth to a dog at some point in the past. However, the Law of Biogenesis states that this was not possible. In addition, every dog that humans have ever witnessed giving birth has always resulted in puppies, never in creatures that were a mix of a puppy and a cat or a puppy and a whale. A brown mother dog may give birth to three puppies: one black, one white, and one brown. But we've never witnessed a dog's mother give birth to anything other than a puppy!

According to the Bible, God said that the world was "very good" once He had finished making it (Genesis 1:31). When God surveyed His world, He was aware that it was the ideal setting for people to develop a love for Him. On day six, he created all of the canines as well as all other terrestrial creatures. Dogs did not acquire new DNA information over millions of years to evolve. They were produced by the same wise Creator that produced humans.

Conclusion

I will conclude this write up with a short poem

Here's what happens:

God said, "They need a friend," as he looked down on his wide-eyed offspring on the ninth day.

Thus, God created a dog.

God proclaimed, "I need someone who will be willing to wake up, give kisses, urinate on a tree, sleep all day, wake up again, give more kisses, then stay up until midnight, basking in the brightness of a television set."

God so created a dog.

I need someone who will sit, stay, and roll over, the Lord stated. Dress in caps they don't need and costumes they don't comprehend without ego or complaint.

I need a boy who can break wind without giving it a second thought. He should also be able to chase tails, sniff crotches, fetch sticks, and cheer people up with a quick lick.

Nobody will judge you no matter what you achieved or didn't accomplish; no matter what you couldn't do, take, win, or make.

Thus, God created a dog.

I need someone who is capable of finding bombs and pulling sleds, yet gentle enough to care for infants and guide the blind, said God. Someone who will spend the day curled up on a couch with a resting head and encouraging gaze to elevate the spirits of the grieving.

God so made a dog.

It had to be someone who, despite loneliness, maintained patience and loyalty. Someone to watch out for, hug, snuggle, nuzzle, cheer, charm, snore, and slobber with, as well as someone to eat the rubbish and chase the Squirtle's.

Someone with the capacity to unite a family through altruism and an open heart. When their best friend suggests, "Let's go for a ride in the automobile," they act like a dog who would yelp, pant, and then wag their tail quickly in response.

God thus created the dog.

Reference

https://apologeticspress.org/god-created-dogs-3216/

https://www.sumasacchurch.com/sermons/joshua-146-15-lessons-from-a-dog-aug-4-2013-pastor-carl-crouse-sacc

https://www.adventistworld.org/seven-things-dogs-teach-us-about-god/

https://hungrygen.com/dog/

Jennifer Far is a missionary partner with her husband Jerry as well as a wife, mother, worldwide speaker, and parent. she has served in the church for more than 25 years. They established the non-profit One-Way Evangelistic Ministries together in Cheyenne, Wyoming.

"Spiritual Lessons from a Dopey Dog," written by Jennifer, is now available. The humorous, fascinating experiences of Roscoe, Cosmo, and Trixie make this a fantastic daily devotional for dog enthusiasts of all ages. You can read it alone or with family and friends to make it even more enjoyable.

Jennifer delights in utilizing light humor and spiritual insights to teach Biblical principles in amusing and helpful ways. She draws inspiration from her three children, Daniel, Rebekah, and Isaiah, as well as, of course, their loving dogs. She only wants people to get closer to God.

Jennifer loves her ministry, travelling on mission trips, and spending time with family and friends in addition to writing.

www.ingramcontent.com/pod-product-compliance
Lightning Source LLC
Chambersburg PA
CBHW060951130726
48001CB00012B/2133